HAIR-RAISING HALLOWE[EN]

SPOOKY

HAUNTED HOUSE

DIY COBWEBS, COFFINS, AND MORE

by Mary Meinking

CAPSTONE PRESS
a capstone imprint

Blazers Books are published by Capstone Press,
1710 Roe Crest Drive, North Mankato, Minnesota 56003
www.mycapstone.com

Library of Congress Cataloging-in-Publication Data
Library of Congress Cataloging-in-Publication data is available on the
Library of Congress website.
ISBN 978-1-5435-3029-2 (library binding)
ISBN 978-1-5435-3033-9 (paperback)
ISBN 978-1-5435-3082-7 (eBook PDF)

Editorial Credits
Mandy Robbins, editor; Juliette Peters, designer; Morgan Walters,
media researcher; Tori Abraham, production specialist;
Marcy Morin, scheduler; Sarah Schuette, photo stylist

Photo Credits
All images Capstone Studio: Karon Dubke
Shutterstock: Sasa Prudkov, cover, design element throughout,
Wandeaw, cover, design element throughout

Printed and bound in the United States of America.
PA017

Table of Contents

ENTER AT YOUR OWN RISK!

For Halloween this year, turn your basement or garage into a haunted house. Your house of horrors will scare all who enter!

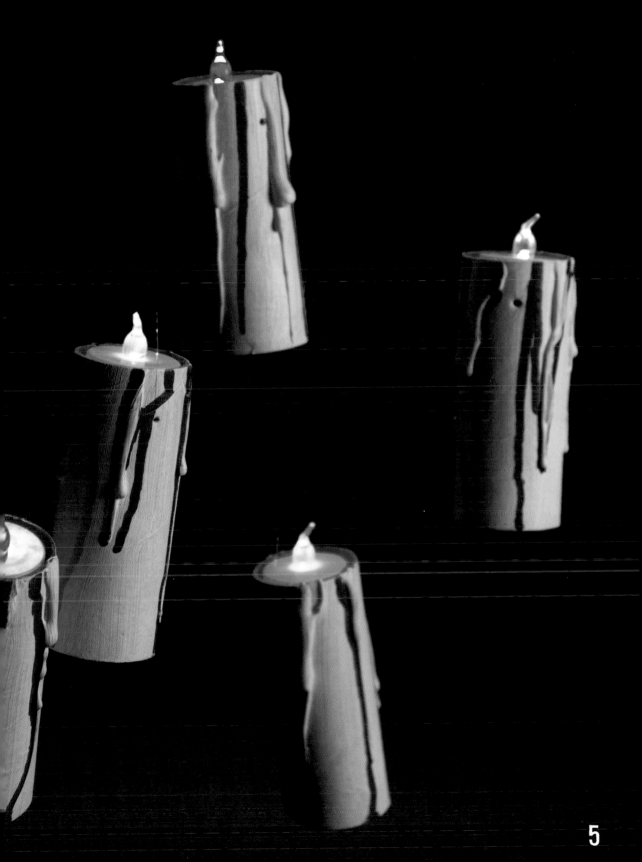

SET THE SCENE!

Follow these tips to get
the most screams.

Map out your haunted house. Plan how guests will go past each attraction.

 Darkness is your friend. Turn off the lights. Block the windows. Cover up the walls with rolls of black plastic.

 Don't forget the finishing touches. Everything looks scarier with cobwebs and fake blood on it.

 Get friends and family to work for you. Some can be terrifying creatures. Others can run the **special effects.**

 Surprise your guests. Unexpected movements get more screams.

 Play scary background music to set the mood.

special effect—an illusion created for entertainment purposes

SPIDER DROP

These creepy spiders are waiting to pounce. They will attack at your command.

WHAT YOU NEED:

- ❑ a metal screw eye for each spider
- ❑ a screw hook
- ❑ fishing line
- ❑ fake spiders
- ❑ a 1-inch (2.5-centimeter) metal ring

1. Have an adult help you attach the screw eyes to the ceiling.

2. Screw the hook into the wall around shoulder height.

3. Tie a long piece of fishing line to each spider. Thread it through a screw eye in the ceiling.

4. Once all of your spiders are tied, pull the loose ends together. Leave enough line to reach the hook. Tie them to the metal ring.

5. Loop the ring around the hook.

6. Have someone hide by the hook. They can drop the spiders when guests come through.

MAD SCIENTIST'S LAB

Set up a mad scientist's lab. You can really freak out your guests with these creepy preserved animals.

WHAT YOU NEED:

- ❏ fake animals (bugs, snakes, frogs)
- ❏ jars with lids
- ❏ water
- ❏ green and orange food coloring
- ❏ vegetable oil
- ❏ antacid tablets

1. Place the animals in the jars.

2. Add water and a few drops of food coloring to some jars.

3. Stir and cover with lids.

4. Fill the other jars ¾ full with oil. Then pour water to 1 inch (2.5 centimeters) from the top.

5. Drip in a few drops of food coloring on the oil. Drop in half an antacid tablet to make the oil bubble before visitors arrive.

Tip:

Arrange your jars on a table. Add some creepy props. For extra spookiness, put a **black light** in the overhead fixture.

black light—a light bulb that shines blue-black light; some things appear to glow in the dark under a black light

FLOATING BLOODY CANDLES

Make candles float in the air. It will look like ghosts are carrying them.

WHAT YOU NEED:

- ❏ hot glue gun and glue
- ❏ empty toilet paper tubes
- ❏ acrylic paint (white and red)
- ❏ paint brushes
- ❏ thumb tack
- ❏ fishing line
- ❏ LED tea lights
- ❏ a metal screw hook for each tube
- ❏ a pencil

1. With an adult's help, drip hot glue down the outside of the toilet paper tubes.

2. Paint the tubes white. Let them dry.

3. Drizzle red paint down the tubes. Let it dry.

4. Use the tack to make a hole in both sides of the tubes at the top.

5. String a piece of fishing line between the holes. Tie the ends together.

6. Place an LED tea light into the top of each tube. Have an adult help you use hot glue to secure the lights in the tops of the tubes.

7. Attach the hooks to the ceiling.

8. Hang the candles from the hooks. Use a pencil to flip the LED light switch on before your guests arrive.

GHOSTLY REFLECTION

Create a haunted mirror. More than a reflection will stare back at your guests.

WHAT YOU NEED:

❑ a large picture frame with glass

❑ glass cleaner

❑ paper towels

❑ a black-and-white print out of a portrait (the creepier the better)

❑ decoupage glue

❑ brush

❑ a can of mirror-like spray paint

1. Have an adult help you remove the backing, picture, and glass from the frame. Clean the glass on both sides.

2. Cut out the portrait. Paint the front of the picture with glue. Stick it to the back of the glass. Let it dry.

3. Have an adult spray paint the back of the glass with several coats of paint. Let it dry.

4. Replace the glass and backing in the frame.

Tip:
Hang a hallway full of creepy photos to lead your guests through.

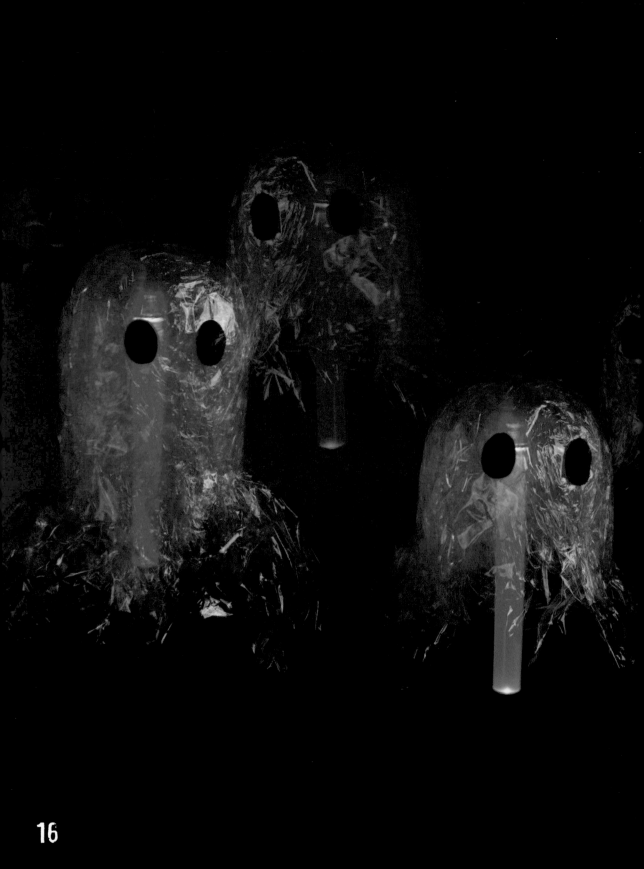

GLOWING GHOSTS

What's a haunted house without ghosts? These glowing ghosts will hover over your guests.

1. One at a time, place each ball on the vase. Cover the top with cling wrap. Leave it hang at the bottom. Overlap the layers.

2. Cover the cling wrap with packing tape. Slide the ball out.

3. Cut out two felt eyes. Glue the eyes onto each ghost.

4. Snip a small hole in the top of each ghost. Poke the top loop of a glow stick through the hole.

5. Put the fishing line through loop. Tie the ends together.

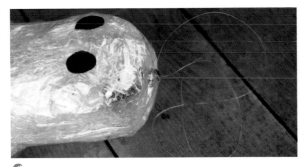

6. Have an adult help you attach the screw hooks to the ceiling. Hang a ghost from each hook. Make as many as you want!

SKELETON-FILLED COFFIN

Watch out! This rotting skeleton is trying to escape from its casket.

WHAT YOU NEED:

- ❏ black spray paint
- ❏ a large plastic tote
- ❏ a scissors
- ❏ a roll of weathered wood grain contact paper
- ❏ black duct tape
- ❏ a black blanket
- ❏ fake blood, moss or dead leaves (optional)
- ❏ a 3-foot (.9-m) tall **poseable** plastic skeleton
- ❏ LED candles

1. Have an adult spray paint the tote and lid black. Let it dry.

2. Cut a piece of contact paper slightly smaller than the lid. Stick it inside the lid.

Continued on next page

poseable—the ability to change positions

3. Duct tape the lid onto the casket from the inside.

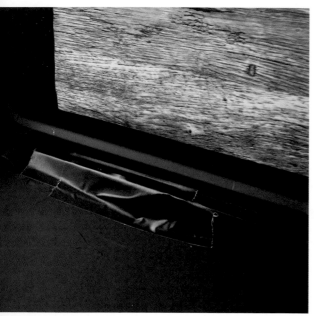

4. Position the tote with the lid open where you would like it to be in your haunted house.

5. Fill the tote with a black blanket. You could add moss or dead leaves as well.

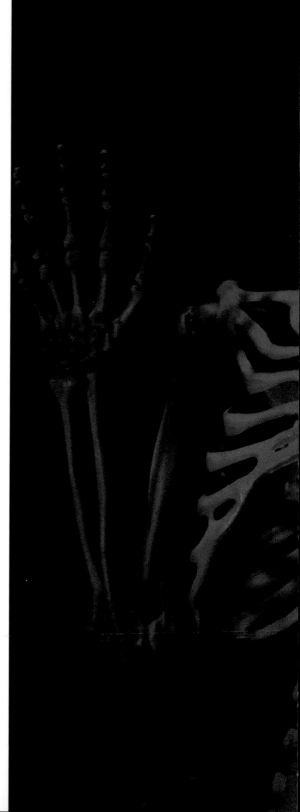

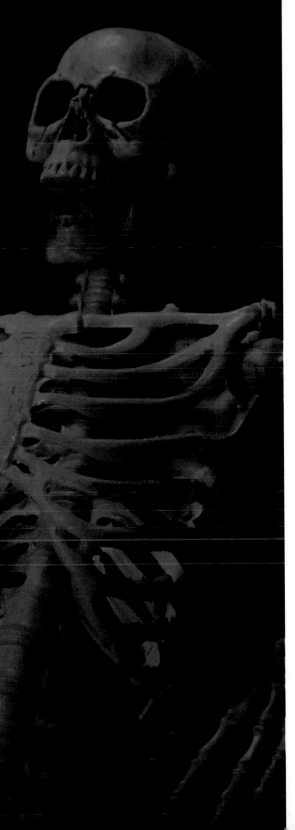

6. Place the skeleton in the tote. Prop it up as if it was trying to climb out.

7. Surround the skeleton with LED candles. Turn them on just before your guests arrive.

Tip:

Add fake blood, bugs, or snakes to your coffin for a scarier look.

ZOMBIE ON THE HUNT

This zombie just escaped from the grave. Put it near the skeleton to create a scary graveyard setting.

WHAT YOU NEED:

- ❏ ½-inch **PVC pipes**
  - 1 straight 6-inch (15-cm)
  - 4 straight 11-inch (28-cm)
  - 2 straight 13-inch (33-cm)
  - 1 straight 24-inch (61-cm)
  - 2 90-degree elbows
  - 2 45-degree elbows
  - 1 cross piece
- ❏ 2-inch (5-cm) pipe insulation
- ❏ duct tape
- ❏ a pair of fake hands
- ❏ a zip-up hooded sweatshirt
- ❏ a 5-galllon (19-liter) bucket
- ❏ gravel
- ❏ a zombie mask
- ❏ a foam head
- ❏ plastic grocery bags

1. Build your zombie's "body." Start with the 24-inch (61-cm) PVC pipe. Add the cross piece. Put the 6-inch (15-cm) pipe sticking up for the neck. Add two 13-inch (33-cm) pieces to the sides for shoulders.

2. Now build his arms. Put a 90-degree elbow on the end of each shoulder. Then add an 11-inch (28-cm) piece on each shoulder. Put a 45-degree elbow on each arm. Then put another 11-inch (28-cm) piece to finish each arm.

Continued on next page

PVC pipe—a white plastic pipe used in plumbing

3. Slip the insulation over the shoulders and arms.

4. Duct tape a hand on each arm. Then slip the hooded sweatshirt over the body. Tuck the end of the hands into the sleeves.

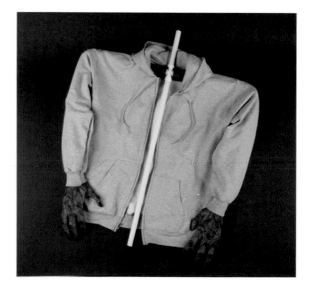

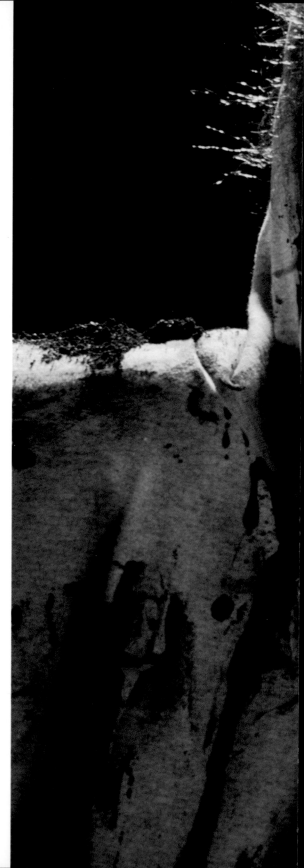

5. Stick the body in the bucket. Have an adult help you pour the gravel around the pipe.

6. Put the mask over the foam head. Push the foam head onto the neck.

7. Stuff the sweatshirt with bags, and zip up the hoodie. You can add fake blood and props for an extra creepy effect.

Freaky Fact:

The first "haunted attraction" opened in 1915. The Orton & Spooner Ghost House was in Liphook, England.

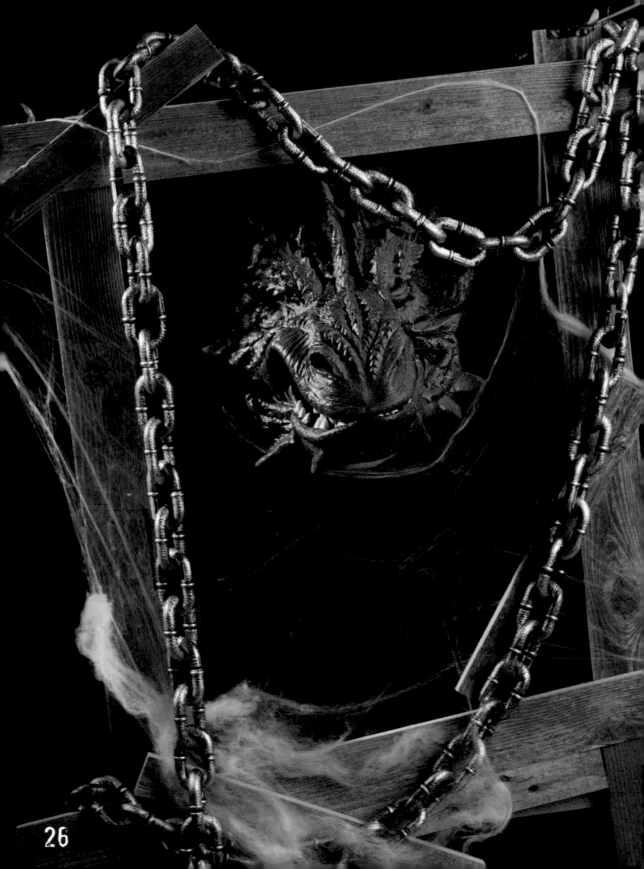

GRUESOME CAGED MONSTER

This snarling, frightening monster is trying to escape its cage. Set him up in a door frame or an open closet off a hallway. It will terrify your passing guests.

WHAT YOU NEED:

- ❑ hot glue gun and glue
- ❑ a bundle of wood scraps (sold at craft stores)
- ❑ a long window screen
- ❑ a utility knife
- ❑ a scissors
- ❑ 1 black plastic tablecloth
- ❑ a staple gun and staples
- ❑ plastic chains
- ❑ an actor wearing a monster mask
- ❑ fake cobwebs

1. Have an adult help you hot glue scrap wood around the screen's frame. Let some of the scraps hang over the edge. This will help it lean against a doorway or closet frame.

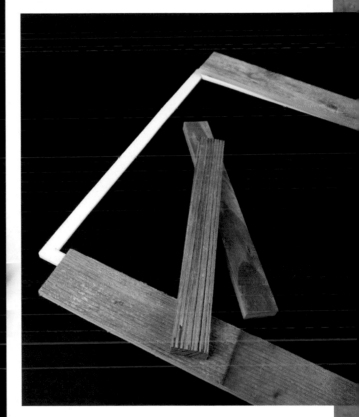

Tip:

Splatter red paint or fake blood on your screen for an added scare.

2. Cut a hole in the screen the size of your monster's face.

3. Cut the tablecloth in half.

4. Turn the screen over. Have an adult staple one half of the tablecloth at the top of the back of the screen. This half will hang behind your actor.

5. Staple the other half of the tablecloth from the middle of the screen to the floor. This will hang in front of your actor.

6. Loop the chains on the cage. Lean the screen against an open doorway or closet.

7. Have your actor stand behind the screen. He should stick his head out the hole. The top tablecloth should fall behind your actor. The bottom half will be in front of him.

8. Ask a friend to put on your scariest monster mask. Drape the mask with cobwebs. Have him scare your guests as they walk down the haunted hallway!

GLOSSARY

black light (BLAK LITE)—a light bulb that shines blue-black light

decoupage (DAY-koo-pahzh)—the art of decorating a surface by pasting on pieces of paper then covering the whole object with layers of varnish

poseable (POSE-uh-buhl)—the ability to change positions

preserved (pri-ZURVD)—when something is protected so that it stays in its original state

PVC pipe (pee-vee-SEE PIPE)—a white plastic pipe used in plumbing

special effect (SPESH-uhl uh-FEKT)—an illusion created for entertainment purposes

READ MORE

Besel, Jennifer M. *A Halloween Drawing Spooktacular!*
First Facts. North Mankato, Minn.: Capstone Press, 2014.

Loh-Hagan, Virginia. *Haunted House. D.I.Y. Make it Happen.* Ann Arbor, Mich.: Cherry Lake Publishing, 2016.

Owen, Ruth. *The Halloween Gross-Out Guide.* DIY for Boys. New York: PowerKids Press, 2014.

INTERNET SITES

Use FactHound to find Internet sites related to this book.

Visit *www.facthound.com*

Just type in 9781543530292 and go!

 Check out projects, games and lots more at
www.capstonekids.com

INDEX

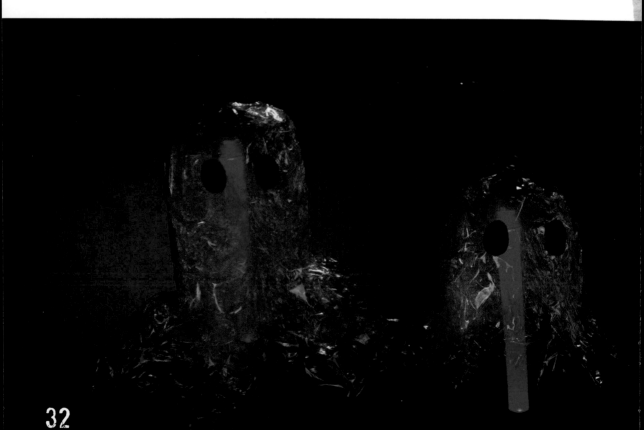